THE ROLLER CANARY

THE
ROLLER CANARY

ITS HISTORY, BREEDING, TRAINING
AND MANAGEMENT

SEVENTH EDITION
Completely revised by
A. F. DEMAINE

CONTENTS

ILLUSTRATIONS

5

1. INTRODUCTION

B EFORE the first edition of " The Roller Canary"
appeared there was little written in these
islands expounding the song or dealing with the
breeding and training of the Roller Canary. A text
book was needed and the former editions of this
book were of great help to those seeking guidance
in Roller culture. The time has come, however, for
a thorough revision of this work to bring it up to
date, enabling lovers of the British Roller Canary
not only to breed and rear this wonderful songster,
but also to educate them in the multiplicity of his
tours and their variations, and thus place them in
a position to appreciate in full the excellent and
good, as well as to condemn the unworthy and
the bad.

In the case of the novice, the help and guidance
gained from his fellow breeders who are familiar
with the tours of the Roller will profitably be
supplemented by what he finds here, and if, in the
light of the explanations and definitions given him
in this work, he studies his own birds at home and
those of others he may meet, it will be a lasting
source of pleasure to him.

" The Roller Canary " is based upon the
knowledge and experiences of both British and

foreign breeders. Tastes differ, experts differ and some may not agree with all that is laid down here, but it is hoped that this book will prove useful and educative, and be of interest to all.

The reader may wonder why foreign words and vowels are used to describe the various song passages. Most of the tour names were manufactured in imitation of the notes of the birds and are of German origin. They are now used universally throughout the English-speaking world. As regards the vowels there are five only in the British Song Standard namely a, e, i, o, u, and the reader will find it easy to familiarize himself with them and their pronunciation which is as follows:

a, is pronounced as a in haha, papa.

e, is pronounced as our short a in mate, rate.

i, is pronounced as ee in fee, see.

o, is pronounced as o in no, so.

u, is pronounced as oo in pool, cool.

There are thirteen song passages in our British Song Standard, which are made of five Rolls and eight Tours, namely Bass Roll, Hollow Roll, Glucke Roll, Water Roll, Bell Roll, Water Glucke Tour, Glucke Tour, Koller Tour, Flutes Tour, Schockel Tour, Hollow Bell Tour, Deep Bubbling Water Tour, and Bell Tour.

The Bass, Hollow Roll, Glucke Tour, Glucke Roll and Water Glucke are high scoring major tours; Hollow Bell, Koller, Schockel, Water Roll, Flutes and Deep Bubbling Water Tour are good scoring secondary tours; while Bell Roll and Bell Tour are in the minor category.

Breeders of Roller Canaries will benefit greatly by joining a specialist club. Details of these organizations will be found in " Cage Birds," together with useful articles on various aspects of Roller culture which appear from time to time. Every effort has been made to ensure that " The Roller Canary " as it now appears is an authoritative and valuable text book and an authority on all that pertains to the breeding, rearing and training of the Roller Canary.

2. HISTORY

OUR Roller Canary, most wonderful of all the song birds in the world, is a living masterpiece of the genius of man coupled with Nature's creation of inherent musical talent and the gift of mimicry. Sometime around 1625 canaries were introduced into Europe by seafaring men returning from the Canary Islands, and are known to have been kept and bred in varying places along the Adriatic coast of Italy. They were brownish-green in colour and slightly marked or mottled with yellow as will be seen in old paintings of that period. They also thrived in Portugal and Spain in the middle of the 17th century where they attained great popularity as family pets.

The song quality of these primitive birds could not, of course, compare with present day specimens, for man had not yet taken a hand in their musical development and a century passed before some of these songsters eventually arrived in the town of St. Andreasburgh in the Hartz Mountains district of Germany. It was here that the birds were first bred solely for song. Their great gift of mimicry was exploited to the full by the invention and use of ingenious contraptions operated by hand, water and air, producing rolling, bell-like and watery sounds which the birds quickly mimicked and gradually absorbed into their repertoire.

With great care and perserverance the fanciers of St. Andreasburgh contrived to improve quality

A typical Roller Canary. The appearance of the Roller has changed little over the years, but a move is being made to produce brighter coloured songsters.

of song. The Nightingale was used as a tutor to impart his tender, plaintive notes and purity and depth of tone. The eager pupils assimilated these virtues gradually, and the fame of the Hartz Mountains birds spread across the world. They

were infinitely superior to others of the now far
flung canary family, which sang a discontinuous and
broken song with open beak. These scientifically
cultured birds sang with beaks closed and from the
throat, bringing great depth with their deliveries
and clear hollow tones in a rolling fashion.
Eventually they became known to the world as
Roller Canaries.

About the year 1820 Rollers were imported into
England from Germany, and quickly became established favourites. To those early British breeders
we owe a great debt, for they continued to import
the choicest blood regardless of expense throughout the 19th century, and established the Roller
cult firmly in these islands where it has remained
unsullied until the present day.

The British Roller of 1955 is second to none in
the world. It has been trained and cultivated here
for more than 130 years, and it is safe to say that
its future is assured, for few people who have really
known the " King of Songsters " will ever exchange
it for other types of canary however attractive
their form may be.

The appearance of the Roller, because of strict
concentration on breeding for song alone, has not
altered much over the centuries and anatomically
it is as near as it is possible to judge to the original
canary or finch of the Islands. A description of
present day colour variations will be found in the
next chapter.

3. COLOUR VARIETIES

IT should be noted that the colour and appearance of a Roller is of no consequence whatsoever at a singing contest. The voice only is judged, and it is the voice only which must be the supreme factor in all breeding. Special classes confined to new-coloured birds are sometimes organized, but these are usually entered with Normals and the Yellows.

The Normal Green

As previously mentioned the primitive ancestors of our present day Rollers were dark brownish-green in colour with slight yellow mottling. This " green " is the colour that instantly springs to mind when picturing a Roller, for it is easily the most frequent colour encountered at contests and in aviaries. In fact the most superb specimens ever heard were, and are still, mostly of this original dark brownish-green colour.

Complete green selfs are common, but usually patches of yellow are visible particularly on the throat which is called the " Bib." Many fanciers treasure birds carrying this distinctive marking. One famous line of Greens in Lancashire and the Midlands have a peculiar yellow " Bar " across the back of the head, which appears with regularity season after season. Tail and wing feathers are often seen in varying shades of yellow down to near-white.

It is the practice with many knowledgeable fanciers, after having bred several generations of lighter yellow birds, to revert to the Normal Green cross to revive stamina and song quality. The " Old Hands " said and still say " The greener they are, the better they sing," and this is a fair and well proved maxim.

The Green Normal is a good looking bird in every way, but many prefer to keep the more glamorous Yellow Variegateds and Clear Yellows, which during the past 25 years or so have greatly improved in tonal quality and have won top honours in open competition on many occasions. The winners of the British Championship in recent years have been :—1950 Green, 1951 Green, 1952 Yellow Variegated and 1953 Yellow Variegated which is a good indication of the validity of the foregoing remarks. The Green Normal is the expression of brown and black melanins or pigmentations superimposed on a yellow ground.

The Variegateds and Clears

This colour group constitutes about 25 per cent of our Rollers and very attractive they look. These birds are the result of the selective breeding of individuals showing much yellow marking until that colour became visually dominant in the stock.

The White Ground Group

In the early 1920s, about a century after the Roller came to Great Britain, the first White birds were imported from the Continent in considerable numbers. A few Whites had been seen here prior to that time, but it is from the 1920s, that our White Rollers mostly stem.

The White mutation had occurred many years before this. Strictly speaking it is not a colour, but an absence of colour. To obtain Whites mate Clear White to Clear Yellow. The result may be 50 per cent White and 50 per cent Yellow, or possibly 100 per cent of either.

The White and Blue

An attractive colour combination which is the result of crossing a Green Normal with a White.

The Blue

This is a slate-blue colour which appears when an expression of black and brown pigmentations or melanins is superimposed on a white ground. It is obtained by mating a Normal Green with a White-Blue. Blues often show white feathers on the tail and wings.

To obtain the best Blues, cross the darkest Green Normal with the darkest Blue available. The result may be 50 per cent Blue and 50 per cent Green, or possibly 100 per cent of either. The aim for Blues is to attain darkness in feather, beak, legs and feet.

The Greens from the above mating are Normals and cannot transmit an expression of the blue colour of themselves.

The Fawn or Brown

This shade is rare in Britain. It varies from deep chocolate to pale fawn, and is the expression of brown melanin only, superimposed on a white ground.

The Orange Ground

As the name implies, this is a deep reddish-yellow ground colour which has been cultivated mostly in Europe and the Americas in recent years and has been imported into England. The shade graduates in intensity from deep to pale orange.

The advent of true-bred Rollers in new colour varieties has been of considerable interest as they have a most attractive appearance. They are gradually improving in vocal quality, but so far no Blue, White, White-Blue, Fawn or Orange Roller has won an open British contest. Several have scored well, however, particularly some Whites, and the future looks promising for this new addition to Roller culture.

4. HOW TO ESTABLISH A STRAIN

THERE is not space in a small book of this character to go into all the details of establishing a strain. I shall, therefore, deal only with general principles, but this should provide a good groundwork of knowledge for the Roller breeder.

There are those who say inbreeding is wrong. This is true if it is improperly followed, but not if it is conducted on rational lines. I am, in fact, convinced that line breeding is the royal road to success, and will contend that anything may be achieved in the way of stock breeding by following out the principles laid down in this book.

How is it possible to have a strain unless one does inbreed? The mating of birds gathered from here, there and everywhere will not create a strain. All the great breeders of Roller Canaries in Germany and England had their own strains, strains that were famous for different qualities of song.

Woerz, a great breeder, says:—" Inbreeding is the shortest way for the safe inheritance of certain, nay, of all peculiarities, and for the improvement of the strain. No breeder can do without it. By its means can faults or imperfections connected with the strain be quickly remedied. But one must keep the inbreeding within bounds, and the greatest care has to be taken in the choice of breeding material."

Breeders such as Rosenbach, Volkmann, Engelhe, Trute, Seifert, Bergmann, Erntyes, Wooje, Jacquemin, Neugebaur, Held, McBride, Beddow, Tielens, Braam, De Bruycker and others who have made great strains, all practised and preached line breeding from one strain.

The End Product

Line breeding on sound lines from one strain, will improve the song of the Roller Canary, and by the same process of selection and mating may the outward form of the birds also be improved. Indeed, it is possible by such a policy to create a strain of Rollers which for song and dominant form will breed true season after season with surprising and pleasing regularity, until the breeder can claim, within the space of several seasons, a super-strain of Rollers.

Let us consider the essential factors. Vigour is most important, and in every description of breeding it is the first essential. Breed vigour into the stock in an intensive form and sickness will seldom cause any worry. In my opinion wild birds are so intensively bred that vigour has prevailed for centuries and the weaklings have long since passed away. Select breeding stock from sound healthy birds. Never breed with weak or sickly ones, and it is possible to line breed for ever.

It is inbreeding in families or flocks that has caused our native songsters to breed so absolutely true for size, shape, colour and marking that the young repeat their inherited factors with regularity. Think of the regularity of marking seen in the Goldfinch, the Chaffinch, Bullfinch, Siskin and other British birds. It is all the result of inbreeding. " Birds of a feather flock together " is an old saying, but there is much in the remark that accounts for wild birds seldom crossing with others of the feathered tribe.

Different breeds of wild birds were developed ages ago when birds were in very limited numbers. If such purity of colour and marking was accomplished by wild birds through consanguineous matings just imagine what can be accomplished by man with scientific selection and mating.

We have not to grope in the dark, for the most difficult problems of breeding have long since been proved by our forefathers, though unfortunately few have followed the wise and clever breeders of old.

The more intensively one breeds the more does one stamp upon the strain the qualities it possesses, and the more potent these qualities the greater the success of the strain. If we take song, it is possible to produce by careful selective inbreeding a family or strain, that will be all-conquering in the contests. But, of course, it must be emphasized that the selection must be on the right lines.

In the same way the outward form of the Roller may be improved, and quite a number of good breeders are now seeking to make the Roller more beautiful so far as outward appearance goes. They desire better shape, size, feather, and colour, and they realize that inbreeding will give it to them.

How is anyone to follow the advice given by all the great masters of the past: " Keep to one strain," unless he line breeds? Immediately strange blood is introduced into a stud away go all the distinctive characters of the strain. He who would succeed with the Roller Canary must inbreed. By strict selective breeding, and keeping a careful record of all stock bred and the performances of the best birds, it is possible to achieve success in the highest degree. The breeder must be both patient and firm, ruthlessly eliminating all sub-standard birds from the stock room.

5. SELECTION OF BREEDING STOCK

JUST as a good start is everything in a race or a battle so it is in the breeding of Roller Canaries. There are two or three points that should be impressed most forcibly upon breeders. The first is to start with birds of one strain, the second to have none but thoroughly healthy birds, and the third is to select the breeding stock and let it be in the breeding room as soon as possible after the finish of the moult in the autumn.

The reasons why? The man who has a successful strain of birds has made it by continued and persistent selection over many years, so that you are, in buying stock from such a man, buying the results of his skill and experience. When birds of varied strains are mated together the result is never, or hardly ever, satisfactory, because the blood does not " nick." Then take health. Birds that are not healthy are useless as breeders as they produce nothing but weak, delicate progeny that is of little use.

Thirdly, when birds are placed in the room in which they are to be mated in the autumn and live in it all through the winter they become accustomed to their surroundings, their food, and their attendants, and the results are infinitely better than when they are introduced to the breeding room only just previous to being mated up. This applies more particularly to hens than cocks.

Those who reside in London, Manchester, Birmingham, Bolton, Liverpool, Glasgow, Edinburgh, Leeds, and other large towns have a great advantage over those who live in country districts, as they are able to attend one or other of the Roller Canary Clubs and by associating with the members learn much as to the value of birds and where the best are to be found. Those not so situated are dependent on the reports of contests which appear in " Cage Birds," and the advertisement pages of that journal.

Buy from the Best Strains

Rollers are no more difficult to breed than other canaries. In making a start the novice who is without previous experience of the Roller Canary should secure birds from a first class strain, but he should not buy the finest, that is, top competition stock, because, owing to lack of knowledge and experience he may quickly reap much disappointment and waste a lot of money.

For the first season or two it is wise to go slow so as to learn not only how to breed and rear the young properly, but also to gain all the knowledge possible as to the song. This knowledge takes some time to acquire.

I have said the stock should be purchased in the

autumn, especially the hens.   It is not always possible to buy young cocks from a good strain in the early autumn, as many breeders will not sell such birds until they have tried them out, and tested their song. It is, however, possible to purchase young hens, and yearling or two-year-old cocks, and the best results are likely to come from the breeding of youth and age.

It is not wise to breed from first season birds only. Experience teaches that the best results are achieved when there is age on one side or the other. If an odd proved good mother is available, then purchase her as a " foster." She will be well worth her keep, for she will rear your precious youngsters in an emergency. Perhaps your finest hen may desert her eggs or babes and then the " foster " saves the situation.

I have written of the advantages possessed by those who live in towns and cities where Roller Canary Clubs are in existence. Introductions and recommendations to noted breeders are easily obtained through the officials of such clubs. The best men in these clubs are always ready and willing to do what they can to help a beginner.

Whether you buy from someone to whom you have had a personal introduction, or from someone whose advertisements have caught your eye, it is wise to place yourself unreservedly in their hands. Tell them exactly what money you can afford to spend, and also what you are desirous of accomplishing. If you are hoping to join the ranks of exhibitors, or if you are only about to indulge in the breeding of Roller Canaries as a hobby without any idea of entering competitions it is wise to let the persons from whom you are buying know just what your ambition is.

There are few fanciers who will take advantage of a novice, that is if he places himself unreservedly in their hands, for they too were once novitiates and understand exactly what is required.

Although the beginner is advised not to purchase first class birds at the start yet he is just as emphatically urged to purchase his initial stock from a first class strain. By so doing he may possibly breed a champion right away, and even if he does not the young birds which he does breed will sell far better, because of their pedigree, than would birds that were mere songsters of unknown origin.

Those who are not able to secure an introduction to a high class breeder should study well the competition reports in " Cage Birds," select a breeder who has been successful and write to him, stating requirements, and at the same time asking him for prices and particulars of birds he may have to sell.

Now a word of caution—don't send money to strangers. If you decide to purchase, deposit the money with the Editor of " Cage Birds," who will hold it until such time as the transaction is complete.

This deposit system protects both buyer and

seller. The buyer knows that his money will not be sent to the seller until the deal has been completed to his satisfaction, and the seller knows that he is certain to be paid when the deal is complete. One cannot always be sure when dealing with strangers that they will play the game. Therefore, make " Safety First " your motto. To the credit of the Fancy, one seldom hears of sharp practices.

Experienced breeders can select hens equally as well as they can cocks. They can detect music in the call note. Depth of song is of the greatest importance, and those who are experienced select those hens for breeding which possess a deep quiet mellow call note.

The advantage of going to a good man, that is a breeder of experience, is that you are buying pedigree and all it carries with it in stamina and song. Stamina is essential, not only because of what it does in the way of power of song, but also because birds from a strain noted for stamina are generally good breeders and good feeders. They are prolific, and tend their young well. Sickly, weakly, delicate birds are of no use to anyone. They are an unending source of annoyance and disappointment. Therefore, in all your buying see to it that you buy healthy stock and countenance no other.

Healthy Birds

Birds that are healthy are bright and full in the eye, their plumage lies close and compactly, they are brisk in their movements, their notes are clear and distinct, and their excreta is firm and of a natural colour. Avoid birds who pass excreta that is greenish in colour and slimy in texture.

In late autumn place stock cocks and hens in large flights or cages, separating the sexes, to enable the building up of vigour and stamina.

To be successful in obtaining fertile eggs, the male bird must be vigorous and strong. He must be given plenty of exercise and at the proper time the diet must be both rich and stimulating. This must be kept up all the way through the breeding season, otherwise the first nest may be good, but the second and third not so satisfactory.

The fact that stock birds are too closely confined immediately prior to pairing with their respective hens is responsible for many failures. Stock males should be given all the exercise possible for some time before mating. Fanciers will have to be prepared to sacrifice a little in song in order to obtain this required condition, for with the greater freedom, exercise and the approach of the breeding season the song often becomes unbalanced and less subdued, with the result that quality becomes temporarily affected.

When breeding time is over they can be retrained with good chances of success for the " Any Age " classes at contests.

6. ROLLER DIETARY

Staple Foods: Rape, canary and a mixture consisting of canary, hemp, niger (inga), maw, pinhead oatmeal, bread and milk.

Fresh Foods: Sweet apple, grated raw carrot, suet.

Green Foods: Lettuce, cabbage, watercress, chickweed, dandelion and shepherds purse.

Egg Foods: Proprietary brands, egg substitutes, or fresh egg food made from:—eight arrowroot biscuits well crushed, or ten tablespoonfuls of toasted breadcrumbs, to one hard boiled yolk of egg. Mix well.

General Diet: Rape, *ad. lib.* Canary kept separate, one teaspoonful per day per bird. The mixture, one teaspoonful per bird three times per week. Bread and milk three times per week, prepared in one-inch cubes with fresh milk poured over. Green food daily. Cuttle fish bone and a pot of pinhead oatmeal should always be in the cage. Fresh water, and in colder weather a few grains of suet. Egg food should be given every other day. Apple and carrot occasionally.

Before Breeding Commences and During Mating Period: General diet with increased and more frequent egg food.

Sitting Hens: Rape and canary only; little green food and a little egg food twice a week.

When Eggs Hatch Out: Rape and canary only.

1st day, no egg food, no greens.

2nd day, saltspoon egg food morning and evening, no greens.

3rd day, saltspoon egg food, morning and evening, no greens.

4th day, increase egg food, give very little watercress or lettuce.

Continue to increase egg food until 7th day, then put on to general diet.

Training Diet: As general diet but reduce green food, eliminate oatmeal, then for three days before contest give rape only, with half teaspoonful of canary daily. Egg food twice daily. On return from contest, give bread and milk and keep quiet for few hours. Continue training diet.

During Moult and Winter Months: General diet, with increased egg food, little suet occasionally.

The golden rule is never to overfeed birds. When acquiring initial stock ask the breeder for his feeding methods. The above diet has been proved to be successful but I am not dogmatic about it. Fanciers generally have different ideas on diet and readers will discover for themselves what suits their own birds.

7. THE BREEDING SEASON

IN former times it was the practice to mate up breeding stock on St. Valentine's Day, and there are some who continue with this practice, but those who are wise do not pair up their birds until the third week in March. This means that the first broods may be expected about the first or second week in April. This gives ample time for four nests to be taken before the end of the season in July.

Many take only three nests. They think more of conserving the strength and energy of their breeding stock than they do of the obtaining of an extra nest of young. They are wise fanciers and much to be commended.

Keep Strangers Away

When canaries are breeding many seem to be very nervous and excitable, and while they are not upset by the presence of one who usually takes care of them, they are quick to notice strangers, and during their presence will stop the work in which they are engaged. This is especially noticeable at the time when hens are feeding young birds.

A good rule is to prevent, if possible, persons going into the breeding room while the birds are nesting. When birds are used to strangers no ill effects arise.

Some fanciers have visitors in their rooms every week, and the birds are used to strangers, thus no harm is done, but when birds are not used to strange voices at ordinary times they should not be allowed to be disturbed during the breeding season.

Never Breed Late

It is a great temptation when one has had a bad breeding season to take " just one more nest," so as to level things " up." More often than not it levels them " down." The early bad luck has possibly been due to the fact that one or other of the parent birds has not been in first class condition, and to take another nest of eggs from them would mean a further tax on an enfeebled and delicate body. Good, or bad though the season be, never breed late.

Many of the troubles that afflict the canary breeder are due to late breeding. Late bred birds never moult properly, the season is against them, and late breeding retards the moult of the old birds. A slow moult, or a retarding moult, is never a healthy moult, and the evil consequences of such are sure to be manifested in the next breeding season. It means impaired health and vitality.

Pairing Stock Birds

There are differences in the ways in which fanciers conduct their breeding operations. Some run two hens with a cock in what are known as double compartment breeding cages. Others, run a cock with one, two or three hens, each hen having a separate single cage, and the cock being put with each hen in rotation. The best results come from individual pairs, but if this is not possible never run more than two or three hens with a cock. If the aim is to maintain the vigour and stamina of the stock, one cock to one hen is the best way to attain that very desirable objective.

Arranging the Cages

The cages may be hung on the wall, or stacked in frames, but when stacked they should not touch each other, and never should they touch the wall. Keep them away from the wall and stack by small screws, and thus avoid breeding grounds for red mite.

The single cages should be about 20 in. long, 11 in. deep from front to back and 18 in. high. The nest pan should be fixed at the back, being hung on a screw and at such a height that the old birds may feed the young easily while standing on the perch, which runs from front to back.

The cage should have two such perches fixed at each side of the nest pan. The seed and drinking vessels should be fixed on the outside of the cage, and there should be a couple of egg drawers, either in the front woodwork or else in the wirework.

One of these can be used for egg food or its substitute, and one for tit-bits in the way of special seeds.

Sand or Sawdust Baths?

Never neglect the provision of a bath pan. Let your birds bathe every other day. It will help to keep them healthy and restrain insect life. In cold weather the water should be slightly warmed.

There is division of opinion on the use of sand or sawdust on the floor of the cage. I prefer the former. Sawdust gets in the food and on the top of the water, and as it is not digestible does a great deal of harm to the young birds.

Clean the cages out twice a week, scatter a fair covering of fine gritty sand on the bottom, and you will meet with more success than if you adopt the other system of sawdust on the floor and sand in a tin or tray. Often the latter is forgotten, and grit is as essential to the welfare of birds as is food. Wash the perches every week. Remember that cleanliness is a great aid to success.

The cages should be thoroughly cleansed before the birds are mated up.

Let Them Be Fit

When the birds are paired they should both be thoroughly fit. Never pair birds unless they are full of life, vivacity, and movement. When birds are quiet and listless in their movements they are not fit to undertake the task of bringing other birds into the world.

As pairing time approaches, with the long days and mild weather, the hens that are fit will be hopping and flying about carrying pieces of fluff, feathers, or other light material that may find its way into the cages. They will be quick and active in their movements, standing on the perches flapping their wings and calling to the cocks.

When these signs are observed in a hen it may justly be concluded that she is almost ready for mating. Make sure all these signs are present. The cocks are generally ready before the hens. But be sure they are ready before pairing is started.

Look at the motions of the stock. The excreta from healthy birds is black with tips of white, which denote the passage of uric acid—the natural process of eliminating this acid.

Signs of poor condition are feathers carried loosely, and birds inactive sitting at the end of the perches with feathers puffed out like a ball. Lack of song in the male birds, no calling from the hens, and looseness in the excreta, which is of a different colour, are other signs. Sometimes the birds have an unusually large appetite for soft food and eat very little seed.

The causes of loss of condition are, of course, numerous, but the principal ones are lack of fresh air, fluctuating temperatures, draughts, insufficient exercise and wrong feeding.

The stock cock should now be placed in a training cage and stood in full view of the hen. As soon

C

as she begins to carry material at the back of her beak and pays attention to the nesting pan she is ready, and the cock should be put in with her. A few mornings later the first egg appears. It should be removed, as should the second and third eggs, and all three should be replaced in the nest on the evening of the third day. If this system is followed the eggs are more likely to chip and hatch together.

The first three eggs should be removed with a teaspoon which has been held in the mouth or hand for a minute or so to take off the chill. The eggs must not be allowed to get absolutely cold and should be placed in cotton wool in a small box until returned to the nest. I do not advise touching them by hand.

When returned on the third night the eggs are nearly cold but get warmed up and start level with the fourth. All the chicks, therefore, hatch out about the same time on the thirteenth or fourteenth morning from the return of the eggs.

The average Roller hen lays from four to five eggs, one every 24 hours, usually in the late night or very early morning. As soon as she is set on her clutch, remove the cock and don't allow him to be seen by the hen.

When one cock to one hen is the rule, I like to leave them together all the time unless it should happen that the cock interferes with the hen during incubation or will not do his bit in feeding the youngsters when they come.

Many beginners make the mistake of introducing the male much too early. If the above procedure is followed less time will be wasted in the long run and the stamina of both birds will not be impaired. In the early part of the season, which is between April and July, incubation is usually a few hours longer than when the days are long and warm.

Nesting Materials

There are quite a number of different materials which can be used for nesting. With the porcelain or clay nest pan, a felt lining is always used, clean dry moss, manilla rope cut into short lengths, and well teazled out. Medicated horse or cow hair, deer hair, clean dry grass, are all suitable materials.

Cotton waste should not be used, as it packs down tight and prevents ventilation in the nest. Another disadvantage of cotton waste or wool is that being so absorbent, the nest will not be very presentable after the young birds reach the age of twelve or fourteen days.

In order best to counter the red mite one should look ahead. Therefore, when the eggs are returned to the nest they and the nest should be well dusted with insect powder.

Feeding Methods

The sitting hen should not be given rich food during incubation. Rape, canary and occasional green food is advised, plus a very little egg food.

The preceding paragraphs lead us to the thought that the youngsters will need feeding, but before discussing their food let me give some advice about that of the stock pairs. The first thing to remember is never to overfeed your birds at any time.

For a month before they are mated the old birds should be given some egg food, or one of the proprietary prepared substitutes every other day, in addition to the daily seed which should consist of rape given as the staple food in the seed hopper and a mixture of canary, niger (inga), hemp and maw seed in the seed drawer or tin. Green food should be given every day and an inch sized cube of bread soaked in fresh milk three times weekly.

In recent years cod-liver oil food has been largely used by fanciers. Cod-liver oil food is like whisky in that it needs to be used with discretion. It should never be fed regularly every day, except to bring very backward birds into condition for the breeding season, or to sickly birds. In such cases it may be used every day, also for a day or two before and after birds come back from a contest.

It may be given to the birds twice a week when they are newly paired, and three times a week during the breeding season or every day if given mixed in equal proportions with the ordinary canary food. During the moulting season it may also be used as during the breeding season. Cod-liver oil food is very heating and forcing. That is why it must be used with discretion, and here I again emphasize the undesirability of over-feeding. Some birds are very fond of soaked seed and will often feed on it when they refuse to do so on the ordinary egg food, or other soft food. Opinions on soaked seed are divided, however. Its method of preparation is as follows.

Equal parts of canary, rape and hemp seed should be put into a big jam jar, covered with cold water, and soaked for twenty-four hours. When it has been soaking twelve hours it should be well stirred up with a spoon, the water drained off, and some fresh water poured over it. After a whole day it should again be stirred, the water drained off, fresh water put to it, again stirred, and drained. Then it is ready to be given to the birds.

To maintain a regular supply one lot should be set soaking in the morning, and another at night each day. Thus, that which is set soaking in the morning will be used the next morning, and the evening lot will be used the next evening.

Green Food

I believe strongly in green food, and fresh green food should be given to the breeding stock every day, except for the first three days after hatching. Watercress, lettuce, chickweed, cabbage and dandelion are all good, but do not use too much of the last, especially after early spring. Green food should always be well washed in slightly salted water before being given to the birds.

Care must be taken never to give frosted green food, and at each time of feeding all stale supplies should be removed from the cages. Many cases of inflammation of the bowels are due to stale green food, and stale egg food. The moral is, let all be fresh. Furthermore, never change the usual items of diet; feed to the youngsters the same food they were given in the nest.

Fixing the Leg Rings

When the young birds are five days old they should be rung. The British Roller Canary Association, the National Roller Canary Society and their affiliated Roller Canary Clubs insist upon all birds bred by their members being close rung. Illustrations are given of how the ringing is performed. The three front claws are put together, and the ring slipped over them, then up over the back claw, which is pressed close to the leg.

Evening is the best time for ringing the birds, as the hens are most restful, and do not try to remove them. It is wise to smear the rings with some excreta when they are on the legs of the birds. This dims them, and the hens do not notice them. It is the brightness of the rings which attracts attention, and causes the hens to pull them off. Watch must be kept for a day or two to see that the rings have not been pulled off.

When the young are three weeks of age, the thoughts of the old birds will turn towards another family, and a clean nest pan should be hung on the opposite side of the breeding cage to the previous one, and nesting material provided. Some fanciers

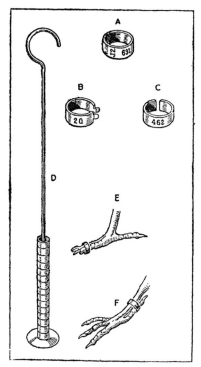

THE RINGING OF ROLLER CANARIES
A. Official closed metal ring, showing letter of issuing organization, year, and serial number. *B and C*. Types of split metal or plastic coloured identity rings. *D*. Wire ring holder. *E and F*. Method of close ringing nestlings.

change the nest occupied by the babes each week, I do not advise this. Even although the nest may become unsightly, leave it alone and avoid disturbing the brood. The only justification for renewal is when red mite are present, and this need never happen if the cleansing and insecticidal treatment are carried out previous to nesting time.

The hen will go to the nest sometimes before her first lot of babes are able to take care of themselves, but the cock bird, if given the opportunity, will generally take charge of the youngsters, and tend them well, until they can fend for themselves. This they should do when a month old, and can then be removed to the flight cages.

A good plan is to place split, coloured identity rings on each bird before placing in the flight. In this way a particular bird can be instantly checked for age, sex, pedigree, etc., and the breeder is saved much trouble.

8. SONG INHERITANCE

NO doubt exists as to the necessity for a tutor in order to educate young birds, although ideas crop up here and there to the effect that education may be brought about without a tutor or schoolmaster. These ideas arise from the fact that in the first place, the bird possesses certain inherited tendencies, and secondly, he will sing his inherited song without ever having had a cock to guide him. This occurs, for instance, if in his earliest youth he passes out of the breeder's hands into those of a person who leaves him entirely to himself, and so permits him to develop his song.

One can adopt an attitude on both standpoints, and correctly so; namely, " breeders need no schoolmaster for song development," and, contrariwise, " breeders are bound to have schoolmasters if they wish to develop their song."

It is asserted in some quarters that even as nestlings, birds acquire already from the tutor the form of their song, but upholders of this theory seem to lose sight of inborn tendencies. If this were so, it would be needless to concern ourselves about pedigree and inherited qualities, and all we need trouble about would be to look out for a good tutor.

We know that we can only produce birds of high

quality from high class breeding stock, yet no one can correctly assert that the nestlings even take up the song of the tutor. It is well known that the father is the best tutor, a fact in favour of our point, for the birds in time will bring out their song, which is an inherited one.

Maternal Influence

There is another example of song inheritance. This is in the case of a hen of a strain representing a variation from the breeder's style of song being crossed with his breeding cocks. The hen transmits, in part or in entirety, the new style of song, but she cannot teach the cocks to sing, so the breeder puts them under a good tutor, maybe their own father. It will then be found that they have not only learnt what their tutor has taught them, but also the pedigree tours of the mother, although they have never heard them.

If the mother is of very fine strain, and the young cocks develop the fine tours inherent in her in the absence of any performance of them on the part of the tutor, it will be evident to the breeder that the birds need no special tutor. These facts have also been further verified in the case of a breeder giving to another breeder eggs from a nest in exchange for a nest of his own, the respective strains being foreign to each other.

Now, if the youngsters hatched in the strange room come from a good Bass or Schockel strain, tours not in the repertoire of the birds in this new home, they will, nevertheless, when autumn comes, bring out their Bass and Schockel, even though they have had no tutor to help them. It is thus shown that on the face of things no tutor is necessary, yet from what follows it will be seen that, in order to obtain a large percentage of good results among the birds, it is necessary they should be coached by capable tutors.

Beauty of Song

The fundamental tours of a canary's song are not the only elements of a good performance, but what constitutes beauty is the order of sequence of the tours, the manner in which they pass one over the other—the bridging over, as it were—the modulation, and the general continuity, for it is all this that goes to make up a fine song and enhance its value.

These special attributes are learnt from the tutor if the young birds are fortunate enough to be brought into contact with a good one. It is through the scarcity of tutors on the one hand, and the excessive number of scholars on the other, that so few birds turn out first class songsters.

When a large number of young birds are on the racks and the tutor is leading, their combined warbling drowns the song of the old bird. It cannot be expected therefore that one single youngster is capable of taking up the song of his tutor when those tours of a quality so necessary for him to study are drowned by the efforts of the large number of birds around him. The result is that, although the tutor plods on his efforts are lost, as not a single cock hears him properly.

If, in order to surmount this difficulty, several tutors are placed among the birds their song will, of course, dominate. As the tutors do not sing the same tour at the same time, but change about, one singing this tour and another that, the result is that the youngster is at the same disadvantage, as the individual tours are lost to him by reason of the strong volume of sound with the, to him, confused interchanges.

Isolated Classes

The foregoing explains the generally indifferent results of large units, notwithstanding the care that may be taken in providing the birds with good tutors. In the smaller breeding rooms there is often a surprisingly large percentage of cocks that develop into first class songsters in cases where they are placed under a really good tutor.

These youngsters have been fortunate enough to have a first class bird to listen to from which they derive great benefit, for although they are with others on the training rack the school is such a small one that their united efforts do not drown the song of the leader. At all times of the day, therefore, he is able to give them direction and support.

If a breeder has a large number of young cocks to train he should not allow more than ten to fifteen for one tutor, and each batch of this number must be kept entirely separate. That is to say, they must be staged in separate rooms, for if these batches are kept in the same room the crossing of the tours both in old and young, will damage the song.

This system of separation into isolated rooms brings the small fancier up against difficulties. He may be able to manage in different rooms so long as the warmer weather lasts, but when winter approaches there is the question of temperature, and for the sake of the birds, which are inactive compared with his hens, and confined to small cages, he may be compelled to bring them all into one comfortably warmed abode. The result will be that the advantage he has gained will be lost, for the birds, although well ahead in tours, are not yet fixed in song and will consequently vacillate and change about.

Power of Mimicry

The imitative faculty of the Roller is remarkable. For instance, time after time it has been found that, in the case of a year-old cock, which has been used for breeding, if when he drops into moult he is placed alongside a cock not moulting, he will take up the new song, so much so that it is often not possible to distinguish one from the other.

In some experiments moulting cocks in a flight were set apart in a quiet room, and here, forming a small undisturbed company, they entirely forgot their own song and acquired that of the bird placed in their hearing. In these cases it was a question each time of a beautifully bent rich song which seems to have been especially attractive to the musical sensibility of the moulting cocks.

If a breeder wishes to obtain the greatest number of good birds but lacks a sufficient number of separate rooms, and, perhaps, of tutors also, let him take the youngsters bred from his best cock and put them with him in a room apart. Failing the parent cock, then some other first class tutor might be used. The breeder may thus reckon on obtaining a small output of good birds.

Where this practice is followed the general stock may be trained in the ordinary way with several tutors if numbers require it, eventually separating those birds that are of exceptional promise and giving them another special room.

9. THE SCHOOLMASTER OR TUTOR

FOR a tutor a quiet, slow, deep songster is better than a bold, racy one. A bird weak in his upper tones is better than one who may sing clear but high, and the bird that starts on his lower tours, Bass for preference, is better than one who starts on his higher tours.

A bird with a faulty high tour or other faults is sometimes good to breed with, if he comes from good stock with a sound pedigree, but as a tutor he is no good.

The tutor should be the best your purse can afford. Many fine birds can be bought at their proper value from well known breeders, but if you limit them to a low figure you cannot expect to get the quality required. The finest birds are really priceless; they are very rare, and their owners keep them. They may sometimes be picked up at shows, but some breeders will not risk sending out their very best for exhibition.

High class birds, however, may be had from fair dealing British breeders which, if not of the very highest category, are of close blood relationship to these supreme songsters, and will, therefore, not only train well, but also breed first class birds.

If the first season does not come up to

expectation, remember it is the second season that generally counts. None can estimate what he possesses until the quality of the grandchildren is known. Perseverance, patience, good judgment, and an attentive musical ear, these are the attributes necessary to a Roller breeder.

One final word as a plea. Take the cages out at least once a day for an hour, and so give the birds an airing and encourage them to hop about and preen their feathers. Make their little lives happy ones, giving them all the liberty and enjoyment that is possible.

Fixing the Song

It is generally conceded that when a bird has recovered his song after the second moult it is fixed for good. There can be very little reason, therefore, why the older birds should not be permitted to enjoy more light and liberty, and live to a good old age.

Now, what are the qualities to seek in a schoolmaster? Upon this hangs the result of our breeding, for after the careful, judicious pairing of our birds, by inattention to this vital question, we can easily nullify our efforts and damage the song through faulty selection of a tutor.

It is immaterial how a tutor commences his song, so long as it starts with a good tone. Some think that a start on the Bell tours may damage the young cocks by encouraging them to sing only light stuff.

This, however, will not occur so readily as in the case of a tutor starting on deep tours and finishing with Bell tours, which linger on as if the bird never wished to finish. Under either tutor there will always be birds who will start with Bell tours.

It is better to have a tutor who starts with a light Bell or Bell Roll, followed, say by Hollow Roll or Bass, followed again by Hollow Bell and Flutes, than one that starts with Bass or Glucke Roll and closes with a Bell that never seems to end. The cocks under the first kind of tutor will almost all start with Bell or Hollow Bell, but they will not make their song with Bell " a yard long." Such a bird gives also a more pleasing effect than the one that starts deep and finishes with Bell, spoiling thereby the effect of the deep tour.

Renderings of Strength and Beauty

Deep, full toned tutors who start with their prime tours will bring often their whole strength to bear on the lighter, easier ones, and these latter will, therefore, always be high if not even sharp. On the other hand, those birds who start somewhere on the higher tours will often bring their strength and beauty to bear on the succeeding tours and so bring the song to a good finish.

Beware, however, that your tutor does not start with too long a Bell, nor must he repeat it. Such a tutor must sing correctly, and without a break or interruption, otherwise the youngsters lose the

D

connecting links and this, when there are many in
school, brings desperate confusion.

It is always best when Bell comes in the middle
of the song; it makes a pleasing change when
followed by Bass or Hollow Roll. To understand
the effect, listen to a songster who drops into a
full round Bass or H.R. after a somewhat high
pitched Bell. To a trained ear this is a delight and
such a bird, moreover, is a good one to make use
of even if his Bell stands out a little too conspicuously in his song.

The next point to consider is what faulty tours
may be permitted in a schoolmaster. Preferably
none, of course. Under this heading I do not refer
to such things as Zitt or Chop, which are not tours
at all but rather jerked out noises, and which
happily only a few birds bring out. Such faults, of
course, no bird should possess, nor any similar.

There are certain faults which we are ready to
excuse in our pets, but they must be sung in the
right place, so that they escape being classed among
the faulty tours. A bird with an Aufzug at the
start is hardly one to be selected. Anyhow it must
be very soft, and he must only bring it once, otherwise the whole school will be spoilt, and there will
be no end to sorting out the birds.

Faults Impossible to Describe

A quiet or medium Aufzug, after Bass or just
before it, may be permitted without fear, but it

must come out only once. The young birds must not be subjected to sharp Aufzug, for after a little while they take up this oft repeated fault, and the effect is bad, like tearing calico. It is impossible to define Aufzug properly in writing, and it is best to listen to an example.

Birds with very lengthy Bell, and which only bring deep tours now and again, should not be used as tutors, neither should those with a lot of sharp, piercing or nasal Flutes, as these birds mar the song to such an extent that it becomes valueless. Weak Flutes will not do much damage and may be permitted, but nasal Flutes are dangerous.

There are some birds that do not have a clear delivery with certain tours half hoarse, half nasal, one might say indistinct. Opinions differ considerably as to whether they are safe to use. A short, indistinct phrase of this character will do no great damage; on the other hand, lengthy Bell and Hollow Bell of this description are very harmful. If one is compelled to use these half hoarse tours they must be short ones; they will always be imitated and made even worse. Really hoarse birds should be doctored in the kitchen or where they can get warmth and moisture.

Birds in full breeding condition should not be used as tutors and the old birds should be taken away during their moult, as they may teach the youngsters many a bad lesson which they otherwise would not get into their song.

10. PREPARATIONS FOR TRAINING TIME

THE flight cages to which the young birds are removed should not be kept in the breeding room, but in another room, in which should be a good schoolmaster, ready to teach the young how to sing. The food given to the birds at this stage should be the same as in the breeding cage, and must be continued right through the moulting period.

It is essential to success in competition work that the birds should be put under the schoolmaster at the earliest age possible. At from six to eight weeks old the cocks may be detected by the swelling of their throats when attempting to sing. They should be removed from the hens and placed in another flight. Some cage them off in small cages, but this is not wise before the completion of the moult as the exercise which the birds obtain in the flights gives them strength and muscle.

Further instructions as to the management and training of the young birds will be found in the chapter dealing with training Rollers for competition.

When the breeding season is over the cages should be thoroughly cleansed by being washed out, disinfected and dried. The room also should be cleaned, including ceiling, walls and floor. The hens may then be kept in this room away from the cocks, and any cocks that prove unsuitable for competition work may be kept there until they are sold, either as pet songsters or for breeding stock. During the winter months the hens and the cocks may be given canary and rape seed as their staple food in the hopper, and the mixed seeds in the seed drawer may be given every other day. Bread and milk, egg food, cod-liver oil food, or one or other of the prepared proprietary foods, may be given twice a week.

Green food should be given whenever obtainable. A slice or two of sweet apple or grated raw carrot may be given when green food cannot be found or by way of a change.

Access to Grit

Let the birds have free access to a grit pan, unless sand is used on the cage bottoms. Keep cuttle fish bone always hanging in the flights. Supply fresh water daily and keep all drinking and feeding utensils absolutely clean. Some fanciers give a little tonic in the drinking water once or twice a week during the moult and also through the winter. Supply them with a bath once or twice a week.

Let the birdroom be well ventilated but avoid all draughts. Thus catered for the breeding stock should keep well.

It is essential for the proper management of a

stud that the recording of the pedigrees of the birds
in a stud register or stock book should be done most
carefully. " Cage Birds " publishes such a stock
book and every breeder who wishes to keep
accurate records should avail himself of the help
it gives.

The daily happenings in the stud may be noted in
a small memorandum book or a card chart, and
then transferred to the stock book once a week or
at such intervals as are convenient.

Beyond its value as a record of the pedigree of
every bird in the stud at any given moment, past
or present, the stock book is deeply interesting and
very helpful, in many ways. It will show all the
pairings, with ring numbers of old and young, dates
of mating, laying and hatching, together with the
results of each nest of each pair and the whole stud
for the season.

If properly kept, it will contain records of all
sensational birds, all birds that have been afflicted
with illness, and also those that have died either
from accidents or disease. All records in connec-
tion with the pedigree of each bird should be
entered fully into the stock book, so that a quick
reference can be made if required.

A small book should be prepared, or a breeding
chart should be made. The most convenient form
is a large thick piece of white cardboard; this can
be ruled to provide a column for each cage, allowing space for three nests from each pair of birds.

The ring numbers of both male and female should be placed in the first square, and as the work of the season progresses, notes can be made in the respective columns regarding results from each pair, such as time set, time due to hatch, number of young birds hatched, and number raised, together with the ring numbers of the young birds themselves in each succeeding nest.

Later, all these particulars can be entered in the stud register, which becomes a permanent record of each year's work. The value of coloured identity rings has already been mentioned.

11. TRAINING FOR COMPETITIONS

THE training of the Roller Canary is, of course, a most interesting process, and occupies about three months, although breeders are not all alike in the time they take to train their birds. One will cage off early from the flights, while another will delay the operation; or it may be that the birds are backward either by nature or by reason of the lack of continual, steady tuition because the available schoolmaster went off song in the moult and no substitute was forthcoming for some time.

It goes without saying that the longer a young bird can be kept in the flight the better chance he has of coming safely through his first moult, of expanding his frame and becoming a robust youngster.

The tutor is kept near the flight in a cage by himself. If a youngster becomes quarrelsome, or if he develops sharp or harsh notes or frequent high calls he should be taken away. To minimize these troubles or to prevent them it will be found effective if the flight is shaded, either by a curtain or by darkening the room.

Some cage off the cocks almost as soon as the sexes are discovered; others cage them off as soon as they show livelier attempts at song. The birds are put into small wire cages and the cages are placed in a cabinet provided with curtains. These cabinets can almost exclude the light, and the birds are ranged so that the tutor is in the centre.

When the young birds are through the moult, place the cocks in the cages, being careful to place the ring numbers on the cages for this will enable any particular bird to be found by referring to the stock book. The training cage illustrated here is the popular all metal type.

A Valuable Suggestion

After placing the birds in the cabinet leave the curtains open at first to make sure they find their feeders and drinkers, and let the curtains remain open for at least two days. On the third day close one curtain, the following day partly close the other, and the succeeding day close both completely.

Be sure to have plenty of fresh air in the room in which the birds are kept. Open the curtains and give fresh food and water the first thing every morning, and leave the cabinet open for an hour. Open the curtains again at noon for half an hour, and then close until the evening.

When several of the young birds are heard singing in the near darkness, open the curtains immediately and let them sing their song. Listen very critically for any bad faults, and when they are finished close up again. The cabinet can be made to any size and is simply a large box with shelves divided into compartments each holding one cage.   See illustration.

Arranging the Training Cages

The birds should be arranged in rows as close together as possible, and if there are many it is

Seen on the right is the popular all-metal type of training cage.   The training cabinet, shown below, is, in effect, a large box with shelves divided into compartments,   each   of which takes one cage, including that of the tutor.

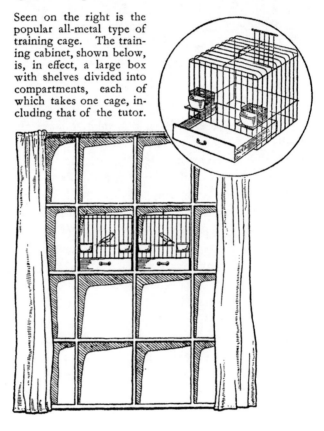

better that the tutor should face them also in his cage. The birds in their wire cages are ranged in racks, bookshelf fashion with two curtains of green casement material suspended in front, one about three inches in front of the other to regulate the depth of shade. If the room has venetian blinds one curtain is sufficient as a rule.

The partition between the cages should be of stout cardboard, thin planed wood, or metal; wood possibly is the best, as the metal is rather cold. These partitions should come well to the tops and the backs of the outside level of the feeding glasses so that the birds cannot get a view of one another. If the cages rest on rods instead of shelves it may be well to lay sheets of brown paper theron, to overhang an inch or so in front and hang down the full depth at back.

Have the upper and lower ranges as close as possible, say half an inch to an inch. In this way there are no cages to clean out, the birds are closer together, can be shifted about more easily and more quickly; in fact they are altogether more easily managed.

Position of Tutor

Place the tutor so that he has two on each side, three above and three below; in all ten birds. Several more can be placed round him, but if this is done it is wise to change the birds about occasionally. If the tutor is placed outside and his light regulated properly, it will be possible to train a great many more.

How to Cage Off

When a youngster is caged off do not shade him at once nor put in the partition; let him get accustomed to conditions for a few days, then put up the partition and, after that, gradually shade him. As the birds are caged off make a note as to their ages; number the cages according to whether they be first, second or third round birds and there will be no confusion over the feeding.

When the birds are opened up in the morning draw out the loose partitions. This makes them active, and they will not sing, or only a little, if at all. Let them have as much of this as possible as it keeps them healthy and happy. Now replace the partitions, and they will start song; close the curtain. Repeat at lunch time.

In the evening, half an hour before roosting time, the partitions may be drawn and the birds left alone until the curtain is drawn for the night, leaving the partitions out. Alternatively, if the days are short you may light up at night and after they have had half an hour's play replace the partitions, draw the curtain, and gradually lower the light.

The shading must be so regulated that although their song is kept subdued they are not stopped from singing altogether. Of course, they will not sing ceaselessly, but the choir will be heard practising more or less during the day.

Now these are not meant for hard and fast rules, but just merely as guiding principles; the idea is to give the birds as much light and exercise as possible, and to use every means, trick or stratagem that can be thought of to keep them from singing in open school, especially during the first few weeks of their training.

A daily rehearsal of ten minutes is good practice, and accustoms them to it. Some breeders rehearse three times. Methods differ but use your own judgment. You will need to study your birds, and you will have them rehearse much longer at times, but this will do them no harm, especially in the cold weather, rather the reverse.

Pupils with Faults

Keep a keen ear and remove any high-pitched offender. If a bird seems inclined that way, put him into a dark corner of your rack. If really bad he must come away altogether, as the faulty tour will vitiate the song of all the others in a day or two. They pick it up in no time, as faulty tours, especially high Bell and, in fact all high notes, are easier for them to imitate than the good deep ones.

Sometimes a bird may not be satisfactory for other reasons. As time goes on his style of delivery may not suit, or he may sing a good tour, but repeat it too often, and so cause it to predominate over the others. That bird should be taken away. He may improve by isolation or placing near another, apart from the rest. Sometimes you may have taken a bird away and may find later on he may go

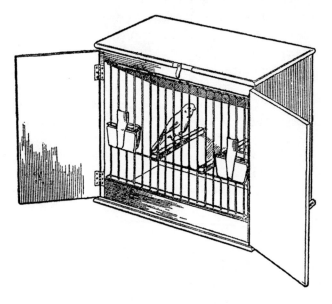

Standard contest cage for Roller Canaries.

back, but when once he has high Bell there is little hope of him being any good in the school.

Keep the best songsters nearest the tutor until they are well advanced. Should the tutor fail you by moulting late, or start early with a long moult, you may find one or two of these youngsters very useful until he comes round again.

When the song has fully developed study the pedigree, find out the lines of the deepest and purest birds and mark the hens, so preparing for next season's breeding. Choose the show birds, transfer them to the standard show cages about three weeks before the show, and train them to sing readily. Shift them about the rooms, move them into all sorts of positions, carry them about to a friend's house, open them out on the table with a sheet of paper before you as if you were judging.

This method ensures that the potential contestants will be well used to noise, movements and unusual sounds, and will stand them in good stead when they arrive at the contest and sing fearlessly before the judge without undue delay. This is a big advantage and much appreciated by the adjudicator who duly notes this desirable accomplishment.

12. THE DEVELOPMENT OF SONG

THE development of the different song tours begins as soon as the young cocks are in the flight cages. They start when they are six weeks old, and in some cases, even earlier. In the elementary stage only a gentle twittering is noticeable, but day by day, it becomes louder and stronger.

The young bird's first moult does not hinder him in this. He practises daily with diligence, and makes progress, and even in these early days, while the birds are still in the moult, one can already distinguish plainly, in some of the more forward birds, certain tours in their song.

Influence of the Moult

If, as occasionally happens, a breeder possesses a young cock who, in spite of being a sound, healthy bird misses his first moult, he will discover that this bird, after a very short course of study, will outstrip his companions, and bring out his tours like an adult. The conclusion is therefore obvious that the moult hinders development of the song.

It is a question of duration—that is, whether the bird renews his feathers slowly or quickly—and it will be found that those which have made the most progress in the moult will show the greatest advance in their song.

Age has nothing to do with it, for birds of the same age who vary in their moult will vary accordingly in their song development. This fact can be verified during any breeding season, for it will be found that older learners having a long moult are outstripped by quick moulting younger ones. With an even moult all round the older birds naturally are the best developed in body as well as song.

As it is mostly the custom to keep the birds in the freedom of the flight cages during the moult, and to cage them off only after completion, it follows that the song develops while they are already in the flights. So long as loud and distinct notes or passages are not distinguished above the twitterings of the beginner, the birds may be left quietly alone.

Faulty Notes

The first of the notes which strike the ear as disagreeable are the faults in the song which, later on, when the bird is fully developed make it necessary to isolate him from the general company. Quite early we may hear sharp Flutes, for these are the first to break in upon the soft warbling. After this we get a lengthy Bell, which gradually becomes longer in delivery and harder, if not finally quite sharp.

E

BIRD SINGING BELL TOURS

Left. Faulty bird singing with beak open.   *Centre.* Bird singing correctly with beak closed.   *Right.* Bird singing with beak only slightly open.

A short soft Bell from which the bird descends to another tour is no fault, and does not jar, but if a young bird brings his Bell frequently and at length the tour almost always develops into a fault, sometimes even a downright bad one, and such a songster may spoil the whole school. By his unceasing ringing he urges on his companions and, as he brings it out by the yard, as it were, nothing but loud Bell is heard after a short time. This long Bell tour may well be reckoned as the worst of all faults, for such a bird thinks he can never do enough of it, and in many cases he will keep it up for pretty well a minute.

Following the above mentioned two bad faults— sharp Flutes and sharp Bell—we very quickly hear the rasping sound of the Aufzug. This is a fault for which most breeders do not isolate if it is not too lengthy, the reason being that with deep voiced songsters this tour of breath recovery will gradually dwindle away. It, nevertheless, has always a jarring effect upon the ear.

Disagreeable Nasal Notes

Then, again, we have the nasal notes. If this fault is confined to a few of the birds, they are taken away from the school, but if nearly all have the fault they will have to be left together. Often when the nasal is first detected it is most difficult to find even one clear voiced bird. For this reason the opinion rules among breeders that the nasal is extremely " catching."

All nasal—i.e. harsh and impure, generally hoarse —tours are very disagreeable, but deep Flutes are the worst when spoilt by this hoarseness. Such birds must be taken away, for this kind of loud Flute is so penetrating in tone that it stands out conspicuously, ugly and persistent, while the others are singing and spoils the effect of the whole orchestra.

The last faults, and most difficult to handle, are known as Schnetter and Zitzit. Loud sharp Schnetter sounds like a loud, hard rattle of castanets, and Bell Schnetter is a sharp Bell, degenerating further into a rattle. Then there is soft Schnetter, which the novice mistakes for soft Aufzug, but which the expert knows is Schnetter pure and simple.

Zitzit is a bad habit which the bird may lose; nevertheless, he must be banished from the school. If he is inclined to let it drop he will have to do so in the company of the other banished ones.

Separate Bad from Good

Birds that have the faults above referred to must be separated from the good songsters as early as possible and placed in another room out of earshot. The chances that such birds may become decent songsters are very meagre. Further, it is waste of time and effort to place them under a tutor. Let them sing their good and bad tours together to their hearts' content, and take the first opportunity to dispose of them as pets.

One is often advised to darken these birds deeply, so as to suppress or stifle the fault, but this will not answer any good purpose, for the breeder who adopts the plan is thereby induced to keep the faulty birds in the same room as the others, thinking that by this means the faults will be less audible. One must bear in mind, however, that the birds cannot be kept in the dark during the whole day. They must at least have light and freedom for one hour every day even if only at feeding times, for then they should have quite an hour of broad daylight accorded to them, so that they may satisfy their needs in a proper manner.

When they are regularly fed, they get to know the time and fidget about from perch to perch beforehand, chirping and twittering the while. When they have filled their needs the little ne'er do wells begin with joy to warble forth their thanksgiving. The signal is given, the band starts and away they go in full strength sharp Flutes, sharp Bell, Aufzug, Schnetter, and all the rest. The performance is so loud and penetrating that the breeder hears it at the other end of his dwelling and hurries off to darken them again, so that his good birds may no longer hear this questionable music.

The best procedure is to place these throw-outs

in a distant room, and let them enjoy life. The breeder, then, has his pleasure in his better songsters far less hindered than when his room contained the blunderers, whose faults even darkening would not completely silence. Having dealt with the development of bad faults we turn our thoughts to those tours which bring joy to the trainer.

13. THE SONG OF THE ROLLER

THE following descriptions of the tours of the Roller Canary, are explained in the simplest possible manner to enable the veriest novice to recognize their salient features. As mentioned previously in this book, all who would know more of the intricacies of repertoire are advised to join a specialist club from which they will be able to obtain much additional information, and those who can attend meetings and contests will have the opportunity of hearing the birds singing and each tour explained as it is delivered.

Hollow Roll

Generally called " The Queen of Tours," probably the most beautiful passage in Roller repertoire, it is classed as a major tour and therefore valuable on the points sheet. The vowels are o and u, and the consonant r. If the vowels a and e are heard this makes the delivery a faulty one. Both the vowels u and o and the consonant r can be heard plainly in most birds and are rendered thus:—
roooroo rooor, the consonant r coming in regularly.

The vowel then changes to the deeper u and becomes rooruuruu, and upon touching the deepest tone gradually rises and goes back into vowel o.

When the bird remains on vowel o such as rooorooroor, and does not drop to vowel u, the tour is known as "straight," and loses value. The whole passage should be unbroken and is best heard when commencing quietly, gradually gaining in power and clarity then trailing off into another tour.

The tone should be full, and mellow, with no watery sounds and can be likened to the soughing wind blowing through a hollow cylinder. It can be rendered in the bottom, middle, and higher middle registers and is most effective.

Bass Roll

This fine Roll is heard only in the bottom register and is the deepest passage in Roller song. The vowels are e and o, and the consonants k and n, with the semi-vowel r. This Roll is also known as Knorre, and in fact the bird actually pronounces this German word thus:—knorrrre, with some power, but it must never be hard.

The Bass Roll is a smooth musical variation. Any suggestion of watery undertone or interjection renders the passage useless, and judges will usually penalize this very important major tour.

Glucke Roll

A major song passage composed of either Deep Hollow Roll or Bass Roll, through which can be heard a fast beating Gluck, Gluck, Gluck, both rendered simultaneously. The vowels of this passage are o and u, the consonants g and r, with semi-vowels r and l. It is usually delivered as oourroouurrr with the distinct Gluck tone heard as a regular quick beating tattoo within the ground vowel tones.

This passage is also of the " dry " variety, the presence of water tones constituting a fault. It should never be hard or harshly rendered, but have a full, round clear and mellow character.

Water Roll

As its name suggests this passage is reminiscent of water rippling along over a stony surface. It consists of vowels a and o with consonant w and semi-vowel r.

The water roll is a pleasing variation and sounds best when it comes in a falling manner thus—woowaaarrrrr. A distinct sound of rippling water is the impression one gets when this secondary tour is heard at its best.

Bell Roll

This is the highest Roll on the song scale, consisting of vowel i and semi-vowel r. It is a minor passage and is delivered as ririri. Often it is heard as the opening passage in a bird's repertoire, but is best expressed when coming as a climax to Hollow Roll as roorouririri.

The bird should not hang on this passage too long,

F

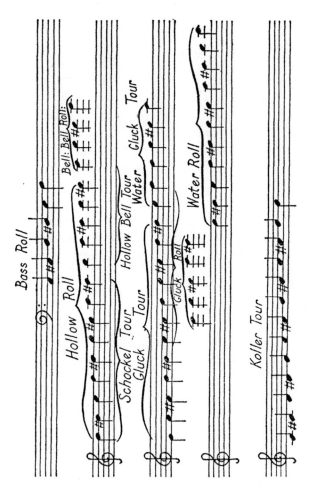

For breeders who have a knowledge of music the
compass of the more valued tours is set forth in
musical notation above.

and it should at all times be delivered in a soft restrained manner.

Glucke Tour

A major tour this, rendered quite dry with no semblance of water present.

In this passage the bird pronounces the word " glucke " clearly and distinctly. The vowels are o and u, and the tour is highly valued when rendered in the bottom register with the vowel u heard clearly in a slow, even beating gluck gluck gluck gluck.

Of secondary value is the vowel o sound, glook glook glook.

If the vowels i and e are heard as glick glick, or gleck gleck, the tour is a faulty one.

Water Glucke Tour

This tour is the opposite to Glucke Roll.   Water Glucke Tour has a pronounced watery undertone through which is heard the distinct Glucke tone, both being rendered simultaneously in either the bottom or middle register.

The vowels are a, o and u, and when this attractive tour is delivered well, the steady flowing or rippling of water is heard, and the beating gluck gluck gluck comes at quick intervals throughout the rendering.

The vowel a sounding glack glack is undesirable, and when the vowel o is heard as glock glock the

tour is of secondary value. The deep u vowel sound
is the aim of all breeders who specialize in this
lovely major tour and those who succeed always
feel well repaid for their efforts.

Koller Tour

This magnificent yodelling passage is very rarely
heard nowadays, but when it appears it is
unmistakable and very impressive, for the bird is
literally yodelling at a rapid rate above a sustained
ground tone.

The vowels are e, o and u with the k consonant
and l semi-vowel. A firm basic tone as rooouuroor
is rendered, and above it the yodelling kollerolleru-
oller is distinctly heard. In fact the word " koller "
is pronounced as clearly as the word " gluck "
can be heard in Glucke Tour.

This tour has also been heard with a water-like
undertone, but always the Koller sound is the
dominant feature.

Hollow Bell Tour

This usually follows the Hollow Roll, and is
likened to a quietly tolling bell. It is comparatively
easy to recognize. The vowels are o and u with the
l semi-vowel, and it appears in all three registers
as ol-ol-ol or better as ul-ul-ul.

This tour has great charm when rendered softly
and evenly, but becomes secondary if the l sound

in the bird's rendering if it is too pronounced.

Flutes Tour

When rendered softly, with a sad or plaintive tone, this lovely tour is an ornament to Roller song and a delight to hear. The vowels o and u with consonants d and h make up this passage, which may occur in top, middle or bottom registers and at the beginning, middle or end of the delivery as du-du-du, dau-dau-dau, hu-hu-hu, ho-ho-ho.

A pleasant delivery of Flutes gives an additional charm to the song as a whole, being a variation separating the sustained Rolls and Tours and preventing any semblance of monotony.

Schockel Tour

An attractive tour heard in all three registers. The impression given is of restrained laughter, and it is often referred to as the Laughing Tour.

The Schockel is best heard as a slightly broken up rhythm; the vowels a, o, u with consonant h make up its composition. Imagine the pendulum of a clock swinging slightly up, down, up, in an arc-like movement, and a fair idea of this passage's rhythm is obtained. The best rendering is hu-hu-hu-hu which is preferred to ho-ho-ho-ho, although the o vowel is also pleasing to the ear.

Deep Bubbling Water Tour

This is best rendered when a sustained watery tone

is heard, and at intervals is interrupted by a bursting bubble effect as bulob-bulob, or bulub-bulub.

It is important that the watery undertone is maintained, and that the bubbling effect is even, beating and clear. This tour in its finest form is becoming rare.

Bell Tour

This is heard always in the top register and sounds very like a tiny tinkling bell. The vowel i and semi-vowel l make up this tour, which is sung by 99 per cent of all Rollers.

The Bell Tour should be clear and even, and sound as li-li-li-li. It is better that the bird does not dwell too long on this tour, but drops smoothly into the Hollow Roll.

Some Faults in Song Deliveries

The Aufzug is a hissing tearing noise as if stiff linen were being torn off in strips. Other faults are nasal Gluckes, Flutes, etc.; piercing, high Bells; sharp interjections and hoarse, rasping utterances displeasing to the ear.

The use of vowels other than those prescribed for each individual tour is another fault, and any water heard in the dry " hollow " passages.

14. JUDGING ROLLER CANARIES

THE Roller judge is a comparatively rare genus. To win his qualifying certificate, he has to have been a breeder and exhibitor for at least five years. Furthermore the B.R.C.A. demands that he obtains recommendations from several judges and finally passes three tests, i.e. practical, oral, and written, before an examining board. His task is difficult and sometimes tedious. He travels long distances, and offends some people and pleases others, but on the whole he is a valuable citizen much to be admired and loves the game for the game's sake.

What is meant when we say " Faults "? We have tried to list them, but have we succeeded in doing so? Long experience has taught that some of those birds which, judged by the list as faulty, are far better songsters than many which are ticketed as " pure," or " faultless."

I will endeavour to explain this view, in the hope that beginners in the Fancy will be guided thereby to think for themselves and not be imprisoned by hard and fast rules.

The listing of faults is useful as a guide, but it does not, and cannot embrace all that should be considered as faulty in a Roller's song. Its great drawback is that it often places a ban on some fault while blinding us to a more serious fault that is not listed.

As an illustration, many novices regard a bird with horror because he has in his song Aufzug, rather sharp Flutes, or a Bell that is delivered rather vigorously, even though it is in the correct register for that tour. Those same novices have looked on another bird as a faultless singer—a bird that, owing to the faulty habit of his song or his thin and " reedy " tone is of no use to serious Roller men.

This because the one fault is listed for the novice to read, and the other and more dangerous one, is not. The latter fault, however, is penalized by every good judge, though it is not in the list of faults. It is penalized by allowing fewer points for general effect. But the novice often does not know that and so is apt to be led astray when considering the relative merits in conjunction with the listed faults.

Definition of Faults

What, then, is the definition of " faults "? There are faults of omission as well as commission. But to avoid confusion, we will define " fault " as something in the bird's song that offends the ear of a judge as being opposed to the ideal.

We all know what sharp Bell, sharp Flutes and Aufzug are, to take the more common of the listed

faults. Let us deal with the faults that are not
listed, and therefore, not so familiar to the eye,
even though they are offensive to the trained ear.
First, there is the bird that gives up eighty per
cent of his song period to the cheap, or low-scoring
tours, only touching at intervals the deeper and
more classical ones.

Every man who has judged Rollers knows these
birds. A bird again and again goes over that inferior
stuff, and at last, when patience is nearly exhausted
he will take a fit and drop down to something of
merit. That is a faulty bird, even though he may
not possess one of the listed faults. Compare with
him a bird who hangs on well to his deep tours,
only very slightly touching the cheap ones; a bird
that pleases you and holds the ear, but occasionally
brings one of the listed faults, not very badly, but
sufficient to gain him a black mark. Which is the
better bird? " Here " says the novice, looking at
the judging sheet " is a faulty bird—and here's
another that is pure, without a penalized point!"
And " bang goes saxpence," or a little more, on the
" faultless " singer.

That novice is going wrong. The one bird, a
grand singer, has one little fault of commission, the
other a serious fault of omission. The one does his
work well and makes a little slip; the other does
his work badly and annoys the judge. The one may
breed and train a champion, the other will give
nothing much better than himself, for if there is

one thing above all others that young Rollers imitate in the tutor, it is this lazy habit of sticking to the cheap and easy tours.

Let us compare now this good, deep, fine toned singer with one little fault with other types of songsters deemed faultless because they have no fault that is in the list of faults.

Compare the bird of thin and reedy tone, beside the other bird as a tin whistle to an oboe. He has a nice range of tours, perhaps, according to paper. He sings no Aufzug or sharp Flute or sharp Bell. He passes without a mark against him.

But his song is a reedy murmur, with no music in it—no " guts," to use an expressive term. There are some who will say he is a " soft " bird, whereas he simply lacks power, volume, tone. As a matter of fact he is not to be compared as a contest bird, a tutor or a sire, with the bird mentioned above with the mark against him.

A Wrong Idea

It is for this reason that some judges oppose the idea that no bird with a mark against him should ever win a first or any other prize when there are these " pure " (so-called) singers in the same class. Having expressed these views I must hasten to add important qualifications.

It must not be understood that I hold a brief for sharp Bell, sharp Flutes and Aufzug. I do not. Nor

do I think that any bird penalized for two faults
should ever be a first prize winner. There is a
vast difference between two and one. The law, as
everyone knows, gives a dog first bite, but he
mustn't take another, or off goes his head.

A really high class bird with one fault is still a
good bird, and a second rate bird with no fault, is
still a second-rater. All things being equal and the
scores level, the unpenalized bird should win, and
that has always been done.

When we hear it said, then, that all winners in
champion classes ought to be " pure " birds let us
think of our definition, remember how many faults
there are that have no penalty column and how
few of those so-called " pure " birds are really free
from even more serious faults than the penalized
bird.

Now we will consider faults in degree, as we
have considered them in kind. What is the degree
of fault that can be forgiven, or when penalized
should not count against a bird winning?

This is difficult to express by any rule of thumb.
It depends solely on the construction of the bird's
song, the tone of the song throughout and the
frequency with which the fault enters that song.
It can be decided on the judging table and there
alone.

It depends chiefly on the extent to which the
fault jars on the ear. A bird that just touches
sharp Bell and then immediately, almost before

the ear has caught it, rolls away on to his deep
song again, possesses a fault that, in a full toned
and deep bird will often add piquancy to his song.
The same applies with a not-too-hard Aufzug, gone
almost before it is there. In another bird, exactly
the same degree of fault, followed by his thin, light
and toneless song, might jar terribly.

The same with nasal renderings. A rich toned,
full sounding singer may touch nasal on some of
his tours, and it will be not at all displeasing, while
a weedy toned bird, on the nasal, makes the judge
writhe. He can only tell what degree of discord
there is when he hears the harmony running with
it. It is the whole song combined that tells him
what the fault is like, and that alone.

Now as to faults in the schoolmaster or tutor.
Very few of the young will escape sharp Bell if it
is in the tutor. It is the same with sharp Flutes,
but they do not always—far from it—bring them
out as badly as they may be in the tutor.

If you train with a bird that has perfect Bell, or
even no Bell at all, you will find a big proportion
of the young come out with sharp Bell; and though
your tutor may have perfect, or nearly perfect,
Flutes, some of the young will take them higher and
sharper. It has been proved again and again that
if you train with a bird that sings no Bell tour,
though the young will develop Bell, sharp sometimes in the training, they will gradually drop it
when their song matures, because not hearing the

tutor follow them, as it were, they begin to follow him. It has been found that the same thing applies to sharp Flutes, when developed in the young, and no sharp Flutes in the tutor bird.

As so many youngsters develop faults even if the tutor does not possess them, is it worth while to put down your champion because he has one fault in his song? For though the pupils may copy his fault, more or less, they will also copy his virtues; and if you use instead that second-rater passed as " pure," you may find yourself still with the fault and lacking the virtues.

A very successful breeder of Rollers once said, " What I look for in a tutor are variety, depth, power of tone and one little fault I never mind."

I don't think I can give the Roller novices any better advice than that.

Faultless Birds Not Always the Best

If a man has the good fortune to possess a champion that has no fault, then he doesn't need advice from any man to use him. But, whether in contests, breeding room or training room, never put back a good bird just because he had one fault in an otherwise grand song and put over him a bird not so good, even though the latter did not commit a fault that could be penalized.

It would mean putting into a back seat many a real champion with one fault and hoisting into premier place third rate birds whose faults do not happen to come into the list where the judge puts down a dot, often with a sigh. He has to let the inferior bird go free, except that he sees it doesn't get many points for its general effect.

It may be said that these faultless (so-called) birds are bound to be good, for, as well as being unpenalized they reach their forty points or so. But that is not the case. A judge has to put down the value of the individual tours when they are sung, however badly those tours are connected, however infrequently the deep tours are heard.

A Rough Guide

The scores of a bird are only a rough guide to his value. His habit of song, his organ-like volume of tone, his steady habit of dwelling on the difficult and hard tours, his contemptuous touching of the lighter tours as something unworthy of him—all these virtues cannot be put on paper any more than faults in the other bird can be listed, faults which make you glad you don't possess him.

Whatever the scores for the individual tours, the judge sees that it is the best bird that comes out on top. Here the " general effect " column comes in.

But what would be the use of all these efforts on the part of a judge to weigh up everything for and against a bird—those good points which are not listed as such, and those faults which are unnamed—if he had to put low in the awards his best bird because it had a penalty mark against him? It would be the end of all good judging, and in time, might well make for the end of all good birds.

As previously mentioned, newcomers to Rollers should join a club if possible, from which they will be able to obtain the precise judging system favoured by that particular club. In conclusion I would remind all would-be Rollermen that in taking up the fascinating hobby of Roller culture they will be accepting a trust carried down through the centuries by generations of fanciers the world over. That trust is " Keep the song in its purity and try to improve it if you can. The voice comes First, Last and Always, guard and cherish it."

Printed in the United Kingdom
by Lightning Source UK Ltd.
132899UK00001B/59/A